Neuro-Linguistic Programming N.L.P. Techniques

Quick Start Guide

©2013 Colin G Smith - All Rights Reserved
www.AwesomeMindSecrets.com

Disclaimer

This eBook is for educational purposes only, and is not intended to be a substitute for professional counselling, therapy or medical treatment. Nothing in this eBook is intended to diagnose or treat any pathology or diseased condition of the mind or body. The author will not be held responsible for any results of reading or applying the information.

Colin G Smith

Table of Contents

Table of Contents 4

PART 1: How To Create Supreme Resource States That Empower You To Make Magnificent Changes.. 5

   NLP Technique: Program A Resource State Into A Future Situation 7

PART 2: How To Make Profound Personal Changes Rapidly And Effectively Using The Awesome Power Of Timelines... 10

   NLP Technique: Reprogram A Recurring Negative Emotion In One Quick Sweep!... 13

PART 3: How To Create A Compelling Future Using The Awesome Power Of Timelines... 17

   NLP Technique: Timeline Great Feelings Into Your Future 19

   Super Simple Technique To Brighten Up Your Future......... 21

PART 4: How To Boost Your Self-Esteem And Much More With The Swish Pattern!...23

   Little Secrets To Make The Swish Easier & More Powerful! 27

PART 5: How To Instantly Gain New Insights, Perspectives And Knowledge That Empower You!..29

   NLP Perceptual Positions 30

   NLP Technique: Condition Your mind To Work In Your Favour 31

   NLP Technique: New Perspectives 33

A Quick Recap 34

About Colin G Smith..36

PART 1: How To Create Supreme Resource States That Empower You To Make Magnificent Changes...

What you will learn:

- What a resource state is.

- How to create a powerful one.

- How to program this into a future event.

I'm glad that you've made the decision to join me as we explore some of the easiest, quickest, and most effective techniques available for creating empowering personal changes.

If you are anything like me, you probably like to learn new and exciting things with a minimum of fluff talk. So I promise to give you a value-packed, clear and concise step-by-step guide that will enable you to become more empowered.

All of the techniques and tools I will show you in this guide are very powerful and useful. Have fun trying them out. That is where you will get most of your learning's from and the more you practice a technique the more your mind will streamline the technique so it becomes re-enforced making it easier to do and more effective!

One of the most important and useful aspects of using NLP to master yourself is in the art of creating resource states. Resource states are states of mind that can be used to positively re-program your past, present and future.

One of the classic uses in NLP is for programming a state of confidence into your future. Most adults have experienced a profound sense of confidence at some stage in their life. Maybe it only lasted a few seconds and was many years ago.

This is fine. The beauty of NLP allows us to capture that wonderful resource and create more of that state, and place it exactly where we desire!

The amount of different useful states of mind is vast and the fact is we hardly ever tap into these 'hidden resources.' Resource states include; Confidence, Creativity, Relaxation, Playfulness, Concentration, Perseverance, Ecstasy.... Any others?

Here's a couple of examples to clarify what I'm getting at:

Have you ever read a book that made you feel really inspired? Where could you use that? How about programming that state into your workplace? Do you compose music? Paint? Giving a sales pitch?

Can you remember or imagine a time being in nature, surrounded by mellow shades of green with soft sounds of birds in the distance and a close by stream. Where could you use that state of tranquillity?

And now to the actual technique. Treat yourself to 10 - 15 minutes to do this the first time. As you practice the technique more you'll be able to achieve good results in less time....

NLP Technique: Program A Resource State Into A Future Situation

1. Think of a resource state you want more of in a future situation. (Joy, Ecstasy, Fun, Creativity, Confidence, Compassion etc.)

2. Relax down into a trance. (Use whatever way you want to go into a relaxed state. e.g. Deep breathing, self-hypnosis, meditation techniques.) The more relaxed you become the more powerful the rest of the exercise will be, so enjoy becoming more relaxed.

3. Remember a time you felt the chosen resource state strongly. Or imagine a situation in the future that would allow you to feel that resource state.

4. Fully associate into the experience and see what you saw at the time, hear what you heard and feel those feelings. Make the colours brighter, turn up the sounds and amplify the feelings. Anchor this feeling by squeezing your finger and thumb together.

5. Notice where those feelings are in your body. What colour would you give these feelings? Imagine spreading that colour/feeling up and down your body, amplifying the feelings. When the feelings are amplified, again squeeze your finger and thumb together to capture that feeling.

6. Break state. (Look around the room or remember your phone number.)

7. Test Anchor: Squeeze your finger and thumb together. If you've done the above steps correctly you should feel those feelings coming back. Congratulate yourself (This is very useful as it re-enforces the idea in your mind that you can do these exercises and they will become

even easier to do!)

8. Here's a great tip they don't often tell you in NLP books. Treat yourself and make a 'Super Resource State'? Go back to step one and stack another state on top of the first one. Squeeze the same finger and thumb together! Cool or what? (Example: Confidence AND Creativity.)

9. Now think of a specific situation where this supreme resource state would be useful.

10. Imagine what you will see/hear just before you want this state to kick in. Example: The boss's door, the eye's of a specific member of the opposite sex, a blank painting canvas, a tennis ball etc.

11. Now fire the resource anchor by squeezing your finger and thumb together whilst imagining being in the chosen situation, unfolding as you desire it too.

Well done, you can now look forward to that future situation even more. Where else and how else can you use the above technique? (Hint: The possibilities are virtually unlimited!)

Each time you practice the technique with another resource state/situation you will condition your mind to make the procedure even easier next time...

In the next part I will show you some of the most powerful & rapid techniques available for programming resource states into many situations at once using the awesome power of timelines. Discover how to re-program a selection of past memories, all at once, so they no longer bother you! How about being able to program a state of courage into a number of specific situations in your future all at once!

Summary of what you've learned:

- What a resource state is.

- How to create a powerful one.
- How to program this into a future event.

I hope you've enjoyed this introduction section . Please do use the technique more than once because this will really benefit you in all aspects of your life. Just imagine what other areas of your life you could improve with just this one technique!

PART 2: How To Make Profound Personal Changes Rapidly And Effectively Using The Awesome Power Of Timelines...

What you will learn:

- What Timelines are.

- How to use them for profound personal change.

- Discover how to re-program parts of your past so it lifts you up.

- In the first part of the course you learned how to create supreme resource states and program them into future events. I'm sure you found it useful and have benefited from that technique.

- In this section I am going to introduce the awesome power of timelines. With timelines you will discover that you can make many positive changes all at once and fast!

- The concept of timelines has been around for thousands of years and is in fact a very simple concept. It was only in recent years though that people discovered, with NLP, how people use timeline concepts to process information (thinking in other words).

- As I want to keep this course as simple as possible, so you gain the most from it, I'm not going to go into how you can illicit your own personal timeline.

- Basically we can represent our personal history and future on a visual Timeline. So we could represent the past going off to our left. We could represent our earliest memories, say 2 meters to our left and then as we go along the timeline it represents more recent times all the way up to our present which would be right in front of us on the timeline. And then we could represent the future going off to the right.

This diagram will make it clearer:

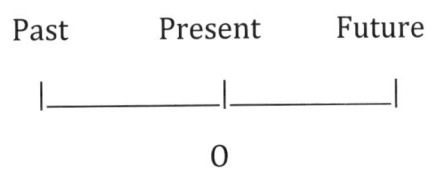

```
       Past        Present        Future
        |_____|_____|
                      0
```

(The little circle is you looking at the timeline)

For some reason some people get a bit hung up on this timeline stuff. "But I don't want to imagine my past there" etc. I used to say similar things until I realised my mind was an incredibly flexible bio-super computer ;¬) You can get your amazing mind to represent information in an infinite number of ways. Timelines happen to be extremely useful.

So just go ahead and try this out as an experiment. I think you'll enjoy it. Once you've 'got' this little concept you are on your way to massive benefits....

Find a room that's big enough to allow you to actually physically walk on the timeline.

Now standing in the middle look in front of you: That represents your present.

Moving slightly to your left is, say a year ago. Move even more to your left and that represents 5 years ago and so on all the way back to being a baby. Play with this until it you feel comfortable with it. You could expand the range or compact it if you wish.

Now come back to the 'present' position in the middle. Moving to your right will place you in the future. Imagine where a year from now is and then 3 years etc. and move to that position.

Notice that at any point on the timeline you can look backwards or forwards to the past, present and future.

Once you've set up your Timeline congratulate yourself. You've just created one of the most powerful change concepts in existence!

Standing in the 'present' position look left at your 'past' timeline and remember a time from a few years ago when you had a wonderful experience. Perhaps it was a memorable holiday for example. Just imagine where that is positioned on your timeline. You may see a vague picture or maybe you represent that time and place with a symbol. You may not see anything and yet you just know where on the timeline that experience is represented; That is fine. Whatever way you know where the experience is located on the timeline, trust it - that's how your mind works and that's great!

Try thinking of 3 memories from different times in your past and notice where they are located on the timeline. Now try imagining a couple of future events. Where are they on your timeline?

Done it? Well done, you're now ready to do an amazingly profound personal change technique....

NLP Technique: Reprogram A Recurring Negative Emotion In One Quick Sweep!

1. Think of a negative emotion that you experience often and would like to change. (Examples: Feelings of guilt, feelings of nervousness, feelings of resentment)

2. Get your timeline set up like we did earlier above.

3. Stand in the 'present' position.

4. Look and slowly walk to your left until you get to the most recent time you felt that negative emotion you choose in step 1.

5. Carry on moving to the left representing earlier times you've had that negative feeling. Go all the way back to the earliest time you can remember this happening. (NOTE: You don't have to get every single time. Lets say eight examples all the way back to the first experience.)

6. Great! Now step back off the timeline and just observe it in front of you. Some people like to look at it on the floor.

7. Notice the memories and how your mind represents them at different positions on the timeline. (Again they could be vague pictures, symbols or just a knowing that they are there. However your represent them, trust your own mind...)

8. Now out of all these examples of times you've experienced the negative emotion what resource state would have allowed you to feel 'normal'? For example if the negative emotion was 'feelings of nervousness', perhaps a state of 'courage' would have been more resourceful.

9. Once you've come up with a useful resource state or indeed states, anchor them onto your thumb & finger like you did in Part One of this guide: "Program A Resource State Into A Future Situation."

10. Let's make this really powerful! Give the above resource state anchor a colour and spread that colour throughout your body and feel the resourceful feelings increasing. Now give this state a sound. Just answer this strange question :¬) What sound does this state sound like? Now hear that sound in your head.

11. Break state: Look around the room or remember your telephone number.

12. Now walk back along your timeline so you are a bit more to your left just before the first time you experienced the negative state you choose in step 1.

13. Look up your timeline and notice the pictures, symbols or 'I just know their there' feelings representing the different times in your personal history.

14. Now trigger the resource anchor by squeezing your finger and thumb together and spreading the colour through your body and hearing that sound in your head.

15. With that resource feeling nice and strong walk up your timeline to the present.

16. Turn around, looking back at the past and imagine the resource colour as a mist permeating and 'colourizing' all of your past timeline.

17. Break state.

18. Think about one of those past memories and notice how your feelings have changed. You remain much more resourceful!

Quite magical isn't it? The wonderful thing about this technique is that not only does it make your past memories more pleasant, it will in fact serve as a powerful inner resource for all kinds of future events too!

You can use this technique for re-programming yourself in many ways. How about re-programming the following feelings:

- Poverty Thinking >>> Gratitude
- Bitterness >>> Loving Feeling
- Irritable >>> Relaxation
- Timidity >>> Confidence
- Over seriousness >>> Humour
- Feeling weak >>> Personal Power
- Sadness >>> Joy

As you use this technique I'm sure you'll imagine many more possibilities....

Keep on doing the timeline technique. You will begin to feel greater esteem for yourself and your overall personal power will increase!

In the next part of the course I will show you how to use Timeline techniques to create a 'compelling future.' You will learn powerful step-by-step methods to program in wonderful states into many future events all at once!

Summary of what you've learned:
- What Timelines are.

- How to use them for profound personal change.
- How to re-program parts of your past so it lifts you up.

I hope you've found this second part of the course very useful. Please enjoy practising the techniques even more because this will really benefit you in all aspects of your life. Just imagine what other areas of your life you could improve with this technique!

PART 3: How To Create A Compelling Future Using The Awesome Power Of Timelines...

What you will learn:

- Develop your understanding of timelines.
- How to use timeline techniques to create a compelling future.
- How to harness the power of your unconscious mind.

In the second part of the course you learned basic Timeline principles and how to use them to rapidly change negative emotions from your past.

Remember this diagram?

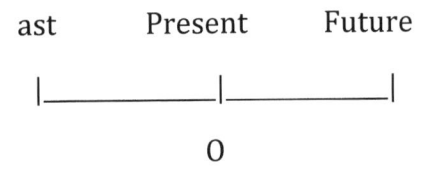

```
          ast      Present      Future
          |_____|_____|
                      0
```

(The little circle is you looking at the timeline)

In this part of the course I'm going to show you how to use Timeline techniques to create a compelling future! You're going to discover how to brighten your future up, program specific resources into future events and harness the incredible powers of your unconscious mind. As Richard Bandler (co-creator of NLP) would say, *"Get ready to be blissified!"*

One of the things that Richard Bandler has discovered as a leader, for over 30 years, in the self-improvement field is that many people often make bad decisions simply because they feel bad too often. When a person feels great they tend to MAKE GOOD DECISIONS.

Feeling good more often has many other benefits including; clearer thinking, optimistic outlook, raised self-esteem, feel more attractive, have more fun and better social interaction....

"OK Colin, that makes sense. How can I achieve that though?"

Well.... below is a technique that allows you to 'program in' good feelings into your future so they happen spontaneously. Have fun!

NLP Technique: Timeline Great Feelings Into Your Future

1. Pick a state you want to experience more of in the future. For example; Fun, Joy, Happiness, Optimism, Faith, Pleasure etc.

2. Remember a specific time you experienced this state. Relax and relive that memory and get those wonderful feelings back. (NOTE: This is what you learned in Part 1: "Program A Resource State Into A Future Situation.")

3. Anchor the feelings to your finger and thumb. If you wish, go back to step 2 and stack another resource state on top of the other one! (eg Fun AND Optimism)

4. Now give this feeling a colour and spread it throughout your being, amplifying the feelings even more.

5. If you could give this state a sound what would it sound like?

6. Break state. Look around the room or remember your phone number.

7. Think of three specific events in the future where it would be appropriate to feel this state.

8. Notice where they are on your timeline. You may see vague pictures or symbols or just know they are there on the timeline.

9. Once you've done that you can allow your unconscious to symbolise other appropriate situations in your future. Trust your own unconscious with this - Remember it keeps you breathing! Go, lets say, a year beyond your 3rd specific event.

10. Now standing at the 'present' position on the timeline,

look at the future and the events you've marked out.

11. Now trigger your anchor by squeezing your finger and thumb together and hear the sound nice and loud in your head. Spread the resource colour throughout your body.

12. Walk up the timeline all the way to the 'year beyond the 3rd specific event.'

13. Now turn around with anchors still triggered and see the resource colour as a magical mist permeating all of your timeline, making wonderful positive changes.

14. Look forward to a great future!

Well done, you've just programmed a 'compelling future.' What other fantastic states could you 'timeline' into your future?

Because the unconscious parts of our minds are so incredible and are the real, 'Captains of the Ship' we can simplify timeline techniques even more AND generate fabulous surprises in the process!

Next I'm going to reveal a very simple technique you can use almost anywhere to brighten up your future.

Super Simple Technique To Brighten Up Your Future

1. Imagine your future timeline going off to your right. You could imagine it going off diagonally or straight in front of you if you prefer. Again your mind is very flexible, experiment....

2. Now looking at your future imagine spreading the colour of 'success' onto the timeline. Perhaps it is glistening gold with silver sparkles. Crank the colours all the way up. Make it brilliant and compelling. WOW - Fantastic! (Be sure to add in some surprise treats. How about some sparkling diamonds?)

3. Add in a powerful sound if you wish. A cheering crowd?

4. Look forward to your future knowing your unconscious has just programmed a compelling future!

This ones great as you can do it almost anywhere. On the bus? The train? Idle time in the office?

Enjoy experimenting with the techniques I have shown you so far. The more you use these tools the more rewards you will get...

In the next part of the course I will introduce you to a very simple and incredibly versatile tool known as the 'Swish Pattern'; a classic NLP technique. I'm going to let you in on some secrets that you don't often get to know about. Little tips that will make 'the swish' easier and even more powerful!

Summary of what you've learned:

- Develop your understanding of timelines.
- How to use timeline techniques to create a compelling future.

- How to harness the power of your unconscious mind.

Well your future is now looking nice and bright, full of fantastic surprises ahead! Be sure to keep on using all the techniques I have taught you so far to get the most value from them. You will benefit in many ways and the tools will become even easier to use with practice!

PART 4: How To Boost Your Self-Esteem And Much More With The Swish Pattern!

What you will learn:

- Discover the basic Swish Pattern.

- How to use the Swish for boosting your Self-esteem.

- Tips and tricks to enhance the power of the Swish.

Today I'm going to teach you an amazingly simple technique known as the 'Swish Pattern.' Many NLP techniques were discovered by modelling what successful people did inside their minds. Before NLP, psychologists and other 'professionals' used to study people with problems and try to work out solutions for them. The developers of NLP thought, 'hmm wouldn't it be better to study people that have had a problem and gotten over it?' They did just that and thus created some of the most amazing personal change tools in existence today!

When they discovered a new way a person solved a previous problem they called this thought process/behaviour a PATTERN. The Swish Pattern uses an area of NLP know as Sub-Modalities. You don't need to know all about Sub-Modalities to use this procedure though.

We actually do 'swishes' inside our minds already below our threshold of awareness. A Swish is a mind process that switches us from one state of consciousness to another. Your mind can swish you to a negative state or a positive state of mind. I'm going to show you how to use the Swish to boost your self-esteem by 'directionalizing' your mind in a positive direction.

The Swish is incredibly versatile with many uses:

- Get rid of unwanted habits such as: smoking, nail

biting, facial tics, nose picking etc.

- Change unwanted behaviours such as: getting angry at people, negative feelings triggered by certain situations etc.

- Change un-resourceful feelings into self-empowering feelings

NLP Technique: The Basic Swish

1. Identify Context: Pick a situation that induces undesirable feelings inside of you? Where or when would you like to behave differently than you do now? (Examples: An interview, Asking someone out, Driving onto a freeway etc.)

2. Identify Cue Image: What do you see in the above situation just before you start doing the behaviour you don't like? Imagine actually being in the situation, seeing through your own eyes. To help get the cue image it can be useful to physically do what you do just before the unwanted behaviour. (NOTE: The cue image can be an internal image inside your mind or an external, real-world image.)

3. Create Outcome Picture: See yourself over there as you would look if you had already accomplished the desired change. Make this image really compelling. How would you stand? What would your facial expression look like? If you had made this change how would you see yourself differently? etc.

4. Swish: Start by seeing the cue image, big and bright. Next put a small dark image of the outcome picture in the lower right corner. The small dark image will grow big and bright and cover the cue image, which will get dim and shrink away. It can be useful to say, 'Swissssshhhh' at the same time! (NOTE: It is very important to do the actual swish very fast for it to be effective: LESS THAN ONE SECOND!)

5. Blank Out Screen or open your eyes.

6. Repeat from step 4 again five times.

7. Test: Now try and picture the cue image again. If the swish has been effective it will be hard to do as the

outcome picture will appear automatically!

One of the great things about this tool is that often the changes generalise into other areas of your life. For example lets say you did a Swish on 'getting angry at partner.' Because the Swish changes your 'self-image', it's quite possible that you will now remain in a more resourceful state in situations with other people whereas before you would of gotten angry!

Little Secrets To Make The Swish Easier & More Powerful!

Tip 1: Identifying Cue Image

If you are struggling to find a cue image you can get your mind to give you a visual symbol instead. Lets say you have an unresourceful feeling you want to Swish. Close your eyes and say to yourself, "What visual symbol represents the unresourceful feeling?" Whatever your mind comes up with, however abstract, use this as the cue image!

Tip 2: Identifying Cue Image II

Lets say you want to use the Swish on a 'low self-esteem feeling' you get from time to time. Imagine the last time you had that feeling or just imagine the feeling now. Notice where those feelings are and then pretend to place that feeling into you hand. Now move your hand up towards eye level and allow an image to form in your minds eye. Use this as your cue image!

Tip 3: Self-Image Outcome Picture

If you are having trouble believing and seeing a you that has made the change you can use a role model instead. "What exactly do you mean by a role model Col?" Good question. A role model is simply a person who you believe has the qualities needed to remain resourceful. The role model can be a real person you know, a movie star or even a character in a book! Remember your mind is amazingly flexible!

Tip 4: Self-Image Outcome Picture II

Because the Swish technique is mainly engaging your unconscious mind, the Self-Image Picture can be vague as long as it feels like a good direction to go towards. Try adding in your favourite colour as a mist around the image and notice how you feel. Or "What colour represents the future you that remains resourceful?" Use that colour as a magical mist. As long as the image feels right and is compelling go for it!

Tip 5: Adding More Power To The Swish

Using this tip is an awesome way to add more 'oomph' to the Swish with a resource anchor. Remember in Part One of the course when I taught you, "How To Create Supreme Resource States That Empower You To Make Magnificent Changes..." The technique where you remember a great state and anchor it by squeezing your finger and thumb together. Yeah?! OK, Great. Stack some resource states together and then trigger that anchor while you create the Outcome Picture in Step 3 of the Swish!

In the next part of the course I am going to introduce you to the power of Perceptual Positions. You will learn how to instantly gain new insights, perspectives and knowledge that empower you!

Summary of what you've learned:

- Discovered the basic Swish Pattern.
- How to use the Swish for boosting your Self-esteem.
- Tips and tricks to enhance the power of the Swish.

I hope this has been very useful to you. The Swish Pattern is one of the best generative change techniques available so be sure to use it on all kinds of things. The more you use it the more good feelings you'll feel towards yourself!

PART 5: How To Instantly Gain New Insights, Perspectives And Knowledge That Empower You!

What you will learn:

- The Perceptual Positions.

- Using Perceptual Positions to re-program your mind for healthier thinking.

- How to gain new insights and knowledge: Wisdom.

Thank you for taking your time to read and apply these learning's. In this part of the course I am going to introduce you to the concept known as 'Perceptual Positions.' You have already experienced this process, probably many times in your life. However learning how to use this concept, with purpose will give you a very simple and powerful tool.

'Perceptual Positions' refers to our ability to view experiences from different perspectives.

NLP Perceptual Positions

1st Position (Associated or Self Perspective)

See the situation through your own eyes. You are primarily aware of your own thoughts and feelings.

2nd Position (Other Person Perspective)

Imagine what it is like to be the another person in the situation. Imagine stepping into their body, seeing through their eyes, hearing through their ears, feeling their feelings and thinking their thoughts.

3rd Position (Disassociated Perspective, Neutral or Meta Position)

Take a detached viewpoint. Imagine you are looking at yourself and the other people in the situation, 'over there'. Try different 'over theres' to gain new understandings.

(NOTE: You can also take the perceptual position of God, Infinite Intelligence etc. for an interesting angle.)

That's it! This understanding is one of the fundamentals of NLP. There are many very powerful techniques that incorporate this concept. In Awesome Mind Power Techniques I've included some excellent techniques that use 'Perceptual Positions' for changing Limiting Beliefs very quickly!

Here's a quick exercise that can quickly condition your mind to work in your favour, making you feel better more often!

NLP Technique: Condition Your mind To Work In Your Favour

Dissociate Out Of Negative Experiences

1. Remember a situation that still makes you feel uncomfortable. Example: An argument.

2. Notice the picture in your mind. Now step out of the picture so you can SEE YOURSELF in the picture, like a movie. (This is the 3rd perceptual position: Neutral Observer.)

3. Move the picture further away and notice how your feelings have changed. You are now in a more resourceful position. "A new perspective" quite literally with nicer feelings! Also notice that you can actually learn more from this perspective. Often people think they have to remain feeling bad about an experience to keep the, 'important lesson.' No, no, no.

4. Do this procedure on three other memories.

As your unconscious mind works very fast it will soon start to generalise this to all your memories! AND it will do this procedure automatically for any future situations...

Associate Into Positive Experiences

1. Next remember a time you had a wonderfully exquisite experience.

2. Fully associate into this experience. See through your own eyes, hear what you heard, smell any smells and feel those great feelings!

3. Fantastic! Do this again with three other positive memories.

Well done you've just 're-wired' your mind to make life much more pleasant!

Next you will learn how to use 'Perceptual Positions' to gain new insights and understandings. The following techniques may radically change your life!

Have you ever had the experience of being in an argument and just being totally dumbfounded by the other persons reactions? :¬))

Or perhaps you've been with a group of people either socially, at work or in a business environment and you don't really understand the other people's perspectives clearly?

The following technique will enable you to gain understandings from many perspectives...

NLP Technique: New Perspectives

1. Think of a time when you were in a situation with other people and you didn't and still don't understand their perspectives on whatever issues were discussed. (Examples: A meeting, an argument with someone etc.)

2. Now run through this situation from 1st Position. This means looking at the situation through your own eyes and hearing through your own ears. Notice your feelings and any thoughts you have about it.

3. Next step inside one of the other people present (2nd Position). Literally imagine being in their body looking out of their eyes. So of course you will be able to see yourself. Notice your feelings as you see and hear from this perspective. Become aware of any new learning's!

4. Now move to 3rd position. Remember this is the 'neutral position.' It's kind of as if you are a camera observing everything. See/hear yourself and the others and notice any new learning's you can observe.

5. Try changing 'camera angle.' You can get almost limitless new perspectives. How about, "Getting above it all?", "A birds eye view?"

If you've gone through the process you'll have new insights into yourself and you will have a better understanding of others too. Sometimes this technique can be quite a revelation, seeing yourself as others see you allowing you to change your behaviour to something more appropriate if necessary.

A Quick Recap

Well this brings us to the end of this NLP Quick Start Guide. I appreciate you taking your time to read it and I certainly hope you have gained plenty from it with loads more positive results to come! Please be sure to keep using the techniques so you get better at them and they will become easier and more useful.

Here's a recap of what we've covered:

PART 1: How To Create Supreme Resource States That Empower You To Make Magnificent Changes...

- What a resource state is
- How to create a powerful one
- How to program this into a future event

PART 2: How To Make Profound Personal Changes Rapidly And Effectively Using The Awesome Power Of Timelines...

- What Timelines are
- How to use them for profound personal change
- Discover how to re-program parts of your past so it lifts you up

PART 3: How To Create A Compelling Future Using The Awesome Power Of Timelines...

- Develop your understanding of timelines
- How to use timeline techniques to create a compelling future
- How to harness the power of your unconscious mind

PART 4: How To Boost Your Self-Esteem And Much More With The Swish Pattern!

- Discover the basic Swish Pattern
- How to use the Swish for boosting your Self-esteem
- Tips and tricks to enhance the power of the Swish

PART 5: How To Instantly Gain New Insights, Perspectives And Knowledge That Empower You!

- The Perceptual Positions
- Using Perceptual Positions to re-program your mind for healthier thinking
- How to gain new insights and knowledge: Wisdom

About Colin G Smith

For over ten years now I have been driven to find the very best methods for creating effective personal change. If you are anything like me, you're probably interested in simple and straight-forward explanations. Practical stuff that gets results! I am a NLP Master Practitioner, writer & author (Colin G Smith) who has written several books and special reports including: *"Creative Problem Solving Techniques To Change Your Life"* and *"Difficult People: Dealing With Difficult People At Work."*

If you found this book useful you will probably enjoy my Amazon Best Seller *"Boost Your Mind Power: 99+ Awesome Mind Power Techniques."*

Please Visit My Amazon Author Page:

http://www.amazon.com/Colin-G-Smith/e/B00A3HEKOM

Made in the USA
Middletown, DE
01 December 2015